The Illusion of Normalcy

Sarah May Butler

Modelbenders Press

PRINTED IN THE UNITED STATES OF AMERICA

Visit our web site at www.modelbenders.com

Cover Designed by Sarah May Butler

The Library of Congress has cataloged the paperback edition as follows:

Butler, Sarah May
    The Illusion of Normalcy
    / Sarah May Butler. – 1st ed.
    1. Teenagers – Psychology 2. Young women – Psychology
    3. Identity 4. Self-acceptance 5. Self-confidence
    6. Adjustment (Psychology) 7. Self-perception
    8. Interpersonal relations 9. Bullying
    I. Sarah May Butler II. Illusion of Normalcy

ISBN: 978-0-9882467-0-6

To anyone who has ever felt like an alien
on their own planet.

Acknowledgements

I thank you, dear Jackie, my soul sister, the one who I would die without. Thank you, Lindz, the most beautiful person I know, the one who loves me even when I don't know how to love myself.

Thank you, Tanquesha and Ida, for changing my life forever; never will I forget you. Sweet Rachel, I love you—just knowing you has allowed me to become a better person.

Thank you, Sarah, for inspiring me with your intelligence and your resilience. Thank you, Mariana—for no one demonstrates the virtue of joy more than you do. Thank you, Marvin, for your beautiful words. Tierra and Tiana, thank you for your compassion.

Nana, thank you for the undiluted love you always give. It is returned. Thank you, Aunt Suzy, for being both an amazing person and an incredible Editor-in-Chief. Papa, thank you for never ceasing to believe in me. Sincere thanks to all of the family and the teachers who enhanced the quality of my passions, who staked faith in me.

A deep thank you to the artists who everyday drive me further over the edge into utter bizarreness, who connect their suffering with mine, who assist me in uncovering my individuality through life; I would not be here today if it weren't for the god Bowie and all the other real artists who speak the painful truth. Thank you to the imparters of wisdom, the writers who blew my mind—thank you, Bob Anderson, for revealing more to me in a couple hours than many others could in a time-span unlimited.

James Marsters, I don't know how to thank you to the extent that you deserve. For you showed me, above anyone else, the beauty in human nature and you made me feel—for the first time—that I am something out of the ordinary.

Thank you, God, for creating love and for giving us souls.

Thank you, dear Father, for never ceasing to push me to be a person of greater strength, greater intelligence, and greater wisdom. No one has taught me more than you have. My beautiful mother...you are the best, the most extraordinary person I know and will ever know. You more than anyone else illuminate to me, every single day, humanity's greatest gift—the ability to love others, *all* others. And Lily love, you are truly my best friend, the utmost greatest, most brilliant part of my life. I wouldn't amount to anything without you.

Table of Contents

1. Foreword

By Bob Anderson, Ph.D., CMSGT, USAFR, (Ret)
President and founder of Back to Basics for Success—
a professional speaking and training organization.

A while back I was privileged to be contacted concerning a new writer. When I received the original manuscript I was amazed at the insight and purpose of Sarah May Butler. In this book, she hits on subjects I have dealt with for years such as "Has anyone ever taught you humility by humiliating you?" "Or, taught you honesty by cheating you?" "And have you gotten a black eye fighting for something you believe in?"

If not, be prepared to now. Sarah is going to challenge you in a unique way to rise to the next level in your life. She demonstrates how we can only excel by going *through* adversity— not by going around it. Sarah has learned strength; she has conquered the trial of being a victim and emerged a victor.

The only way to sharpen a knife is to rub it against something harder than it is. The same is true with people in her case—the sharpening steel was "the populars".

Be ready to be challenged and inspired. My philosophy has always been simple: "We can't always control our circumstances or the decisions that other people in our lives make; but we can direct our destiny. It is the challenges we face— not our successes—that define our lives. It is the fears we conquer—not the comforts we enjoy—that define our character. We should always be striving for excellence, and if we don't—we have chosen mediocrity. Legacies are not built by people living in mediocrity. True wealth cannot be measured by dollars and happiness should not be based on what you have—but who you are."

Sarah personifies this concept.

2. Introduction

I am overwhelmingly repulsed by anything and everything that represent so-called normalcy. While this statement may be arrogantly bold as well as an ambiguous generalization, I greatly identify with it. Three years ago, however, I was singing a drastically different tune; as an effervescent but understandably sophomoric middle-schooler, all I desired was to be an essential part of the society of normal acceptation: a highly-esteemed popular teenager. However, if I have learned anything from experiencing my first two years of high school, it is this: normalcy, as well popularity, is banal; they are vapid and uninspired. A series of shattering letdowns and countless diminutive heartbreaks have taught me this much.

The whole, all-exalted state of being *normal*, along with its vivid attractions and lauded lure is nothing but an illusion. It appears to be an impervious verity, as tangible as a playing card. But this playing card, when exposed and turned at the right angle, reveals itself as thin and indiscernible; its meaning has no substance.

Society, for better and for worse, exists in order to limit people, to set standards and rules to restrain them from breaking barriers, from absconding the commercially-constructed boundaries. Yet the most effective way the world imprisons people is through illusion. Modern society has heavily elaborated the crucial nature of being normal, being popular, being right in coats of tediously painted "must dos", "must haves", and "must bes" that the media brushes over again and again.

Normal injected us with a syringe, numbing us against what we subconsciously are already aware of—the fact that normalcy can't satisfy. True, with the normal comes the security, and an expectation that lives languidly upon the couch, predestined to fate. But, normal lacks something that is truly essential, life's variety and vitality—beauty. Despite what the modern manner of living connivingly seeks to advertise, beauty is not an image. Beauty is life's bizarrity—aesthetic dreams, often crazed, even somewhat deranged, that express the value in our flaws and how these flaws define us.

True beauty, according to today's society, lacks in that it doesn't display fundamental symmetry, which is today immaculate in the public eye. Yet true beauty does not claim flawlessness, only an ardent nature. It cannot be defined, is not that simplistic, but must be translated by manner of story. The story may be literal, such as presented in literature or film, or it may be the story of a song, the story behind a smile. The terrifying reality of the degradation and exaltation that comes with living—how this reality bonds with human emotion—this is beauty. Incorrigible feelings exposed, brutal honesty, corporal relationships—these are examples of profound beauty.

That is why when I hear a senseless song playing on the radio that demeans the aesthetics of being human, or when I see a person callously rejecting another for exhibiting strangeness, I ache in despair. Because the special ones, the different ones, these are the beautiful people.

Personally, I reject normal, because normal rejects beauty. And it rejected me.

3. The Loneliness of Rejection

"They cannot scare me with their empty spaces
Between stars—on stars where no human race is.
I have it in me so much nearer home
To scare myself with my own desert places."
Robert Frost

"All great and precious things are lonely."
John Steinbeck

When I was younger, I didn't see the world as an assortment of groups, a variety of segregated peoples intermeshed. I saw people as people, bound by an indubitable pact to care about each other, just because they were all part of the human race. My vision, however, was opaque, and limited by the veil of ignorance that only dissolves as childhood starts to ebb. Now I know what is simple and generic knowledge.

Every group of people excludes others. Even abandoning the big picture, with the boundaries of countries, religions, races, and classes, there are always the popular groups and the sub-popular groups. Human nature tends to exclude, to isolate, to reject; every person in this world is at some time or another treated in this manner. Every human has also subjected this kind of treatment to another.

But never do you see exclusion, rejection, and isolation as strongly prevalent as you do in high school, where many are victim to this treatment by the groups who deem themselves popular. It may be verbalized or taboo, but either way, it tangibly exists, daring anyone to try to question it. It can't be bothered; it just is. And its existence wouldn't pose a problem if it wasn't held together by irrevocably exclusive glue.

There is little more degrading than being blatantly rejected, deemed too negligible and irrelevant to be a part of something "better than you." And even if you aren't outright told that you aren't good enough to be a part of the popular group, its treatment of you surely speaks for itself. This rejection leads to inevitable feelings of uncertainty and turns self-worth askew. You attempt to defend your status, yourself as an individual, but the popular people possess a weapon—they are society's darlings.

How can you resist these feelings of uncertainty when the media manipulates human ideals through television, magazines, and online articles? How can you remain perfectly

3. The Loneliness of Rejection

secure with yourself as you are when the radio blares these messages endlessly, in a redundant stream of this-is-all-that-matters-to-the-world-nowadays, bleaching the minds of Americans to the point that even the basic, most vital principle of humanity is hazy—the contrast of right from wrong. In this day and age, what truly defines what is ethically acceptable? When is cruelty considered to be taken "too far?" Flawless forms, excessive competition, ruthless envy, egocentric ambition, and vanity blind, deafen, and drown our universe...can we trust our eyes anymore, our ears?

How about our minds? Should we resort to our own instinct to make decisions or should we follow the most celebrated world view, collapsing beneath the masses?

The first time my heart broke, I aged a year or two. I asked myself, through the misery of my crippled condition, why my childhood had lapsed into a nostalgic and embittered sepia slideshow. But the fade from the fantastical dream of childhood to the harsh, morally and emotionally draining ache of growing up had been anything but sudden; years elapsed before I realized that the more I had been swallowed into what everyone spoke—their words shadows of what social entities stated as truth—the more I grew into a state of self-defacing insecurity.

For this reason, as we eventually mature, uncertainty begins to tyrannize us, causing us to acquiesce to what we feel is truth; our images and identities are staggeringly different than those who live elite and who society favors. We are made to feel inadequate, unwanted. Self-worth becomes a major factor in our lives as we grow through our teens, because many of us are not what they tell us we must be in order to be relevant to this world and those of it. Despair at failing to meet the standards is now our society's epidemic. So where is the panacea? To lose purpose often means to allow feelings of unworthiness to amplify into a world of loneliness and—in my case as well as the case of many, many others—extreme depression.

Everyone is forced to suffer this way, in this brutal state of assumed worthlessness, at some (usually many) points in his or her life. The main factor that separates these people is what they do with themselves upon being excluded and cast aside. Below is only one story of someone who suffered the rejection that we all have once.

$\sim$

What Truly Matters

At one point in their lives, almost everyone wants to be, in some shape or form, popular. What people don't realize is that the popularity they search for is just a name. As a young girl, being popular meant everything in the world to me. That is, until the realization kicked in that there is nothing special about it. People who classify themselves as the "populars" are often misunderstood kids with huge insecurities so, in order to mask their insecurities, they create a clique. The real definition of popular is being well-known and well-liked because of your people skills, but girls and boys don't have to create a social status to make them feel safe and loved.

Luckily, as we grow older, our insecurities and cravings for popularity fade away, allowing us to make friends that we may have never made. This might make it seem that popularity isn't an issue in this world, but it is, because the insecurities and envies of popularity can lead to bullying. Usually, when a person tries to enter the popular group, bullying arises.

When I was younger, I tried to join the popular group, but they never gave me a chance. I always heard them making fun of me behind my back, excluding me from circles and the lunch tables, calling me names, names that were dogs' names because they associated me being that low. I saw and heard everything. Eventually, I wanted to kill myself, but I never did. Something always kept me grounded; it wasn't my time to leave the world.

Finally, I realized that it was time to stop trying to make friends with people that I would never like. I never enjoyed talking to them. So I made new friends, friends who loved me. The life I lived was pleasant and enjoyable once I found out that it was much better being with people who would open up their doors and give me a chance. So, the point is, why try to be with the popular clique if you are not going to have fun. Be with the people who you love and your insecurities will eventually melt away! Do what you love not to be accepted, but to be happy!

Anonymous

~

Some people overcome the rejection, as seen in the experience above, but unfortunately this is often not the case. Rejection stems loneliness, which leads one to feel hollowness at the lack of relationship, but secretly yearn for solitude. This loneliness tends to cause the misunderstood to delve into the invisible world, because reality's impetuous hand raises stakes which hold far less mercy than the utopia of fantasy. What else is there to do when what is tangible torments and does not bring satisfaction into sight?

Because I couldn't meet the standard, I went into shut down, residing in quietude within my unworthiness; I wasn't living. Fantasies and illusions proved to be like morphine to my depression, providing only temporary release. It is usually impossible not to fall victim to fantasy when you are unsatisfied. It brings out the best of what we want our lives to be and, for the time we lose ourselves to our reveries, causes the undesirables of our lives to fade into the backlight of our subconscious.

However, a false sense of reality cures nothing in long-term; fantasy is the incipient wish of what we dream to be, and indulging in it distracts us from what is. The more I found myself susceptible to fantasizing, the greater I knew the sense of futility in my life was.

It's a terrifying revelation, that sometimes what we live for is a facade. To re-immerse ourselves into that faultless realm comes naturally to us. The more I indulged myself in fantasy, the more complex and intricate my roots in that world became, until I could no longer distinguish what was surreally bound to my subconscious from the bright, agony-infused life before my real eyes. The extent to which I fantasized, the extent to which I started to lose myself to fantasy, became unhealthy. My relationships with the people of the real world suffered due to my infatuations.

Because I believed I was worthless, I thought I deserved to be isolated. I didn't consciously strive for solitude, didn't initially aim to push others away; my self-loathing did that for me. Because I did—I hated myself. I hated that I was considered invaluable, un-ideal, and unwanted. Marked by diffidence, I tortured myself, hurt myself, secluded myself because that's what I believed I deserved. And insecurity is so easily perceived that others can sense it on you upon sight; those who lack the confidence to love themselves are instantly targeted. People take advantage of the insecure, using them because they know that often there won't be any consequences in doing so.

When you're deeply insecure, you won't seek assistance when you're abused or taken advantage of. Usually, you accept the abuse, allowing it to ingrain within you and alter how you perceive yourself. You suffer in silence, living a facade—believable or not, relative to how good an actor you are. You masquerade you aren't dying inside, that you don't have a death wish, that smiling as if the mere transition from hour to hour doesn't cause ache isn't difficult. This isn't posing a fight or survival. This lifestyle is the act of self-induced surrender; it's deterioration. It's dying.

During the time I lived without living, it wasn't lucid to me that the manner in which I walked my days was effectively killing me. I suffered through the fatiguing years and they were the worst of my life, because I hated myself through and through. I lived on the brink of death, of ending it all. Yet all it took proved to be a single individual to change all——to alter my staid life and my view of myself, forever. One person, one that I looked up to and deeply, deeply valued, told me that I was special, and my chaotic spin toward death turned in the polar opposite direction. I began to care about living again and I began to try.

Instead of surrendering to what is unalterable, seize power over what you have power to control. It often isn't possible to change the feelings or beliefs of others and if people are resolute in resenting you, they will. It is difficult to change that. If instead of aiming to change other people's outlooks you work on improving your own, change will happen. After my life turned around, I worked on embellishing on passions, elaborating on what both God and my experience had given me. I found outlets for the dissatisfaction I had in my existence through arts and relationships. And for every person, this is crucial—an outlet into which he or she can express the ugliness of this pain and transform it into something that is far from unsightly.

It wasn't due to my mere audacity or perserverence that I could achieve any type of metamorphis. No one in this world possesses enough internal vigor that they can last this life in loneliness. Looking to end my solitude, I identified the differents from the followers.

It is easy to distinguish a unique person from a mass of un-identities. In the movie Schindler's List, every audience member's eyes immediately fasten on the little girl in the scarlet dress, which is the rare splash of color in the black and white movie. The producers purposely portrayed the girl as wearing the only main color throughout the film, employing her as a symbol for the vitality of her character and the representation she bore of the Jewish community's innocence, despite their persecution. In connection, those who are strange people are glaringly obvious amongst off-hand shades of black and white, and they hold value that their persecutors cannot imitate.

Many a year elapsed before I, a certified weirdo, realized my relevance. I almost involuntarily fall back into previous patterns—those patterns from the days of when I didn't know enough to know what truly makes someone significant—patterns that scarred me too deeply to ever recover from. We choose to let the others degrade us, convince us that we are nothing, and shove us into our dirt, as if they don't have their own. As if we are lesser people, we submissively fall into our roles as the subservient, the victims. We wouldn't be condemned so if we didn't believe we deserved to be. So, the illusion of who we are remains unaltered, and we remain lonely people.

Despite what I know, it often seems the loneliness is never truly evanescent; it always returns on another day. So overwhelming, it obscures rationality and sensibility. And without confrontation from a superior state, never will it leave us be.

∼

Loneliness

It's a leech that drains your hopes to grey
And cold that gnaws your soul to frays,
Arrives without reason then suddenly fades,
The subconscious fear you can't evade.
Tears can't burn its grasp to ash.
It appears out of nothing, a lightning flash.
Stings more than sorrow and numbs more than pain,
It is standing coatless in the rain.
It is watching loved ones from afar,
It is never knowing who you are.
It is letting him touch you because it doesn't matter,
It is watching another relationship shatter.
It is utter surrender or chasing kite-like dreams,
It is nothing being as it seems.
It is disappointment and deflated esteem.
It is slowly ripping at the seams.
It is the despair of being always ignored
And the hollowness you feel when you can't cry anymore.
It is the razor you seize when you're on the brink,
It's the void that can't be dissolved in a drink.
It is getting what you want but never what you need.
It's prayers unanswered for years so you can't concede.
It is staying up by the phone, but nobody calls.
It is blurry faces in the halls.

It is caring too little, too much for everything.
It is surviving by lyrics your mind constantly sings.
It is the monotonous work you can't ever post-pone,
It is being surrounded by people, but completely alone.
Loneliness is a colorless sun.
It is felt by all,
But shared by none.

SMB

Loneliness is, without a doubt, the saddest shade of sorrow. And when experienced, it infects everything that we do and are. When I'm lonely, I breathe into music, art, and writing for release, because I am reinvigorated and reinvented by what I love and what I love learning to know. Each person has something that liberates him or her from loneliness, and allows them to feel what the world attempts to distract us from—the innate sense of who we are, individually and in connection with others.

Whatever we abscond to when reality seems deranged can be classified as an outlet. It has the power to transform us from viewing life as indissoluble to viewing it as underrated—precious and ephemeral. Our outlets provide us with enough passion for living to allow us to hope.

Irreconcilable with loneliness, hope is polar opposite in a survivor's mind. Hope is more prevalent than loneliness, because even when we are at our all-time low, we don't refrain from hoping. It is how we survive. Hope is sometimes all that secures us, all that keeps us sane. While holding hope, we cannot dwell in the hell of lonely. Holding hope, we have to know that there is so much more to life than merely coping with it.

From asking different people, I found that to everyone, hope is different. For all, hope is a touch of brilliance, but to each person it is felt in a particular and unique way.

Hope is—
having something to look forward to.
the light that gets people through life.
what we want through our own pain.
knowing somewhere deep down inside of you that no matter how dark or long the tunnel is, there will always be light at the end if you keep walking.
what you can count on when the rest of the world gives up on you.
a brand of happiness.
knowing that things can and maybe will go wrong, but that there is still a chance that they will also go right.
an earnest, wishful state of mind.
believing that your greatest desire will come to life someday.
expecting the best, even in the worst of times.

To me, hope is what prevents you from abandoning life, what counters negativity. Alone, hope is not enough. But when exorable, it creates the blueprints of transformation, allowing the birth of dreams. For without dreams, hope alone will not suffice.

4. Desiring Popularity

"Do not spoil what you have by desiring what you have not;
remember that what you now have was once among the things
you only hoped for."

Epicurus

Popularity–
Wanted, desired.
Lying, pretending, delusion.
Only be a select few
Approved.
Tierra Barfield

A dictionary definition of popular is "appealing to the general public; well-liked," and for this reason, it might as well be "sought after; desired." If you are not included in the popular clique or viewed as successful in society, you will at some point in your life, as it is a condition of human of nature, long for this approval. In my past, I craved and to be accepted, particularly...and didn't believe another way existed that would allow me to possess self-worth.

"Nothing" was the world I enchained myself to everyday, because most people made me feel like that was, in essence, the word that fit me best. And I absorbed the lies, those ugly tags they nailed me with, because my tormenters were great in number, and I felt like a solitaire. Succumbing to their treatment of me, in a sense I joined them in their criticism of me. I agreed with them, because I *was* inconsistent with what the world declared I should be and I didn't fuse into the rest. I couldn't even if and when I tried. So I hungrily swallowed their lies.

Like so many, I suffered for the crime of being myself in a world of actors. My peers attacked not only my face and my physique, but my personality and what I believed I stood for at the time. *Hideous*, I was called, *weird* and *worthless*. The girls my age mocked me, saying I resembled a boy, and the boys treated me as if what the girls claimed was irrefutable. My interests varied from theirs, and though I tried in vain to conform, they called me *freak* as if it were my name. Their taunting ranged from being vague and generalized to agonizingly specific. When I was younger, I struggled with bad skin, and the people my age mocked me for it and said I looked like a leper. Humiliated for too long, I started wearing makeup to attempt to cover my flaws and they laughed at me, saying I looked like a clown. My ardent pursuit of my studies caused them to label me as a nerd. I tried to act normally, and they reasserted the truth that I was anything but; I tried to look normal, and they went out of their way to tear me down, criticizing my hair, my nose, my face, my body. I was too naive, too introverted, and too insecure to stand up for myself, and at the time, there wasn't a soul there to stand up for me.

It's shocking and saddening how cruel we can be. Even young adults (*especially* them), even children. Bullying overwhelms thousands of people, but is found most often amongst teenagers. According to bullying statistics, the bullying epidemic has led over fourteen percent of high school students to consider suicide. Seven percent attempt it. Many teenagers endure not only verbal abuse, but physical. And more often than not, almost always, this bullying is exerted by those who love to refer to themselves as *the popular people.*

It isn't a sin to feel this desire to belong, to blend into the rest so that you won't have to be a victim of torment. No matter how brazen the person, all human beings long for security and many abhor change. Most treat what they don't understand as repugnant. Having people in your life that are intrigued by what sets you apart from others, and not repelled by it, is imperative.

Even disregarding the bullying, I know that the times in my life when I most needed acceptance from the crowd was either before I found friendship with those who unconditionally accepted me for who I was or when I was in the midst of a rough patch with said friends or family.

You aren't, in any respect, disparaging or unappreciative for doubting relationships, circumstance, and life itself doesn't make you disparaging or unappreciative in any respect. I personally have, at different times in my life, longed for people outside of my zone of acquaintances to have relationships with, because I believed that the current people in my life didn't know me to the extent they should, didn't fathom who I was.

At the worst of times, this proved true; I hadn't yet found people who loved me as I was. But even after I had, this longing, though milder, didn't abandon me. In this case, it wasn't my friends who didn't know me well enough—they knew me well for who I was at the time, incomplete, unfinished. I possessed the potential to be more than I was, to begin to gravitate toward who I am meant to be, but because I hadn't yet realized the truth of this and I didn't respect myself due to my insecurity, I didn't seek out to better myself.

When you don't know absolutely who you are, when your identity is like a mirage—you think you know who you are but one day, whether gradually or in a revelation, you discover that you don't—you are eaten alive by desire. Once I came to terms with who I wanted to be as a person, only then could I start to genuinely care about myself and find incredible people who genuinely cared about me in return.

Only then did my desire begin to dissolve, until now, at the present, it is barely existent, the skeletal remnants of a want that once controlled my life. Desire for popularity and acceptance once dictated my life, shoving every other goal I had into the dusty backdrop. Now my desire burns, more immense, for greater cause and truth.

The most dangerous threat I indulge in is taking for granted what I have, all the amazing people and experiences I've been privileged to be a part of. In many ways, this is my Achilles heel. I often utterly overlook the positives of my life, engulfed by the negatives, forgetting to appreciate the beautiful people that surround me, lost in longing over those who aren't a part of my life.

We always want what we don't have; whoever claims reverse is selling something—we want it all. I had to learn through the most basic and grueling way, through raw experience, that seldom could I be a part of *that* group, be in connection with her or involvement with him.

At the brink of teenagedom I once stood, expecting to be given the world, expecting to continue to be loved as I was in childhood: just for my kindness, just for my smile—just for myself. But we aren't given so much, not *that* much at all; instead, like every other semi-child, aging forced me to stare down the tracks of a hundred crossroads. We are privileged with personal choice before we are privileged with the knowledge of how to choose. And the problem with this is while we always choose the road we think we want, it rarely runs parallel to the one that we need.

Basically, in youth we are granted power, but without the wisdom to utilize it—that is, properly, to our long-term benefit. When we choose to seek acceptance, to accommodate ourselves, not to benefit ourselves or others but to benefit an image, it is a decision governed by our will-power, our want-power, but falls short of our true potential. It is an equally argued and refuted scientific theory that human beings only utilize a small percentage—ten to twenty percent—of our brain power. In the same way, many people, teenagers as well as adults, only utilize a diminutive percentage of our power to be unique, to be genuine, to be creative. Fitting in isn't normalcy and normalcy isn't reality. Reality is that the less we seek to fulfill an image, the more we will benefit ourselves and others—the more we will benefit humanity.

Despite our power to choose, the limited control we do possess over our own life proves to be for the most part lost in terms of events outside our own actions. The only element of control we are able to exercise in situations outside of our individual grasp is our response to them. While more often than not, hopes and prayers aren't answered instantaneously, it often seems to work that when I least expect or hope to obtain what I'd dreamed or prayed for, it may then be offered to me. Occasionally everyone will be given that one ideal that he he or she desires, that object of your affection; this could be called a blessing. But rationally, more often than not, acquiring what we think we most want, most desire, doesn't occur— not within a short span of time. Long-term goals are named such for a reason. All we can do at present is ensure that they are the right goals, and then work toward them.

Mere words won't assist a single soul in ceasing to desire the unattainable if he or she doesn't begin to make the steps away from this preoccupation themselves. I never stopped longing after that guy, that group, or that achievement when similar words were spoken to me; it was not redundant words that resolved me to tear myself away from this unshakeable yearning.

Knowing what is true can cause dawning that otherwise would never have been obtained. If you do know, in some surreal, partially conscious manner, that you are blessed for the people you have, the truth of what you are insecure about will spark in your vision with clarity. When this occurs, I have learned that it is less arduous to discover what it is about my life that causes me to feel unsatisfied with what I have and desire to be involved in what is outside my grasp.

Desiring popularity is desiring acceptance, approval, a polished self-image. When what you see is what you lack, nothing but obtaining it possesses you. If you see yourself with more clarity, you can see what absence is splintering your esteem.

If you not only thrive but live on the security of being labeled "popular," of being surrounded and overwhelmed by semi-genuine friends, then *you* are the one who is deeply insecure. The girl alone on the outside, who appears cumbersome, with the unorthodox attire and a flamboyant attitude, is likely the one who is secure with who she is. The boy with only a friend or two, who dares to shine in academics, is the one who will go far in life. And in the long run, *they* will be the happy ones.

If you are truly different from the rest, you will never be incorporated into any clique. If you possess a mind that the world would define as a hazardous collection of hues of madness, if you aren't moved by commercial lures of products that have no significant purpose, if you perceive this world as such a deeper phantasm than what materialistic people attempt to sell, then you never will be graced with the embrace of popularity in your life. In most cases, the nature of popularity can be characterized by commercialism, abiding by the trends just because the headlines declare they're "in," and acting superficially simply because you aren't impassioned enough to seek out your own identity. A mask is far safer than an emotion-riddled face.

Take yourself aside and consider—what would you rather? To endure the ignorant, malicious behavior of others for being as you are—vastly peculiar, your own original—or to dilute yourself, blend like watercolor into the million shades of grey. Seeking to go halfway exists as an option—to be a split personality of superficial and real, fake and strange—only in short-term and only in theory. Every time you present yourselves to others, you have to opportunity to choose who you want to be. From experience I know not to straddle the cumbersome fence between both sides; living that way, I was never happy.

Superficiality aside, the people who claim to be popular are, more often than not, the people without identity who project their insecurities into varying facets of pride, arrogance, and malice. They lash out at others, specifically the different people, and are, strangely, admired and worshipped by the vast majority for doing so.

I must clarify that in reference to "the popular people," I am not referring to the entire body of people who are accepted by the majority. If you are accepted, well-liked, that means you are privileged, because your life will liable be easier than that of those who aren't so welcomed. There is no sin in the state of acceptance; in fact, to be accepted is to be blessed. It would be incredibly hypocritical and prejudice to resent others for this reason; in some cases, they deserve to be admired so. I have met kind-hearted people my age and otherwise who were widely accepted for their genuinely friendly and humorous nature. It may be excruciatingly difficult to deal with the fact that the accepted are treated as if they are "above you," but they don't deserve to be resented for being so. Popularity holds a different connotation than merely being the subject of mass admiration.

Popularity is characterized by one accepting and believing that he or she holds more value to the world than others do. It always goes hand in hand with the development of a superiority complex, viewing others as inferior, and usually leads to that individual purposefully deriding people, especially the socially unaccepted.

When people desire to be a part of the popular clan, they desire to be a member of a group of genuinely insecure, emotionally disillusioned human beings. For those who proudly claim this name not only exclude others, but often torment them as well. By doing so, they aim to distract themselves from either their lack of goals, lack of values, or lack of purpose, but all they do accomplish is to force themselves further and further away from the hope of being a genuine, compassionate person.

Popularity is an institute, a fad built on indifference. Usually, the less you care, the more you are considered and acknowledged. That doesn't mean indifference to what people think of you—that type of indifference should be embraced to a level in order to survive in a sadistic world. Yet the more you sweat blood over what the rest think of you, of every step of life that doesn't work out as you planned, the more fatiguing and demanding your life will be. Coming from a person who worries about issues as trivial as losing the ball in soccer or or a mediocre test grade, this may come off as hypocritical. But many others and I would gladly atest—it is truth.

Yet popularity takes indifference to an entirely different level, respecting those who project the image that they don't give a damn about anything but the present, anything but themselves. People say that in relationships, whoever cares the least has the most power. This may be true, but it is also delusive.

The person who cares the least is the one who receives the least out of the relationship. Why be in a relationship that doesn't incite growth? Why live in a world and not truly revere any aspect of it outside of yourself, not benefiting from how it has the power to move us to laughter or tears and the willingness to let us learn to fathom it. Disregard power and success; reevaluate morals imperative to becoming a person even more valued than who you wished to be.

By permeating the sometimes opaque illusion of popularity and gazing beyond what the majority of society sees when they flatly observe these people, conception of exactly what it is the popular people are and stand for can be breached. And when this is accomplished, it isn't unlikely that the desire will burn a little less susceptibly, even to the point where it will cease altogether.

They say, Here's the lock. Now fit into it. The majority willingly comply, warping themselves, their bodies, their personalities in the process, in order to force themselves into that tiny lock. Some are required to cut themselves down into a less complex and less intricate person, while others are complient with growing themselves out into a larger than life character, but all are utterly resolved on achieving that status that society deems perfection—when the key fits. Now thousands of keys fit the lock, millions, with a click. Once they click, society sighs. Now that's better—you're normal. You're right. Congradulations—do you feel better—grounded and self-assured? It's liable you do, as it's what you're programmed to believe. Be an automaton. Be akin to everyone else.

But you don't have to do that, you know…shrink yourself down to their level…blow yourself up into someone you're not. Fitting the lock isn't what they tell you it is—it requires no talent, no purpose; it's what's expected of you…and anything but difficult to acquire. Jamming the lock; for it's confounding the mechanism by not connecting with its required code—now that's talent. Now that is pretty damn special.

The courage that it requires to not be another easy fit, and the beauty, the uniqueness that's needed in order to do it—it's breathtaking. It's what blows people's minds, changes their lives. It's different; it's the difference that causes the change.

5. Searching for Identity

*"Most people are other people. Their thoughts are someone
else's opinions, their lives a mimicry,
their passions a quotation."*
Oscar Wilde

*"Those who dream by day are cognizant of many things
which escape those who dream only by night."*
Edgar Allan Poe

Identity. It could easily be the answer to all questions that
hold relevance, could dexterously tie into any conversation
regarding human confusion. In order to make any critical life
choice, you must possess some sense of who you are, some
embryonic sense of identity. However, most people don't discover themselves until much later in life. Teenage years are so
emotionally sapping and wrought with anguish because we

teenagers are expected to assume responsibility and execute decisions when we aren't fully sure of who we are as human beings yet. And uncertainty can often lead to anguish, and even worse, a threat of sanity, as seen below, in the poem of a teenager who fights society's shallow standards.

∾

Am I truly sane?

In my sanity am I truly sane?
Or are my eyes blinded by the possibility
That this society is trying to kill me?
Its strategy is to keep me busy with ambitions filled with vanity,
Compare life to a fantasy
Then attempt to live it like a movie.
This is a cycle
Viciously recycled without remorse,
On a course towards tragedy and like plenty of people
My dreams are haunted by past sins.
Hear the screams of my heart being terrorized by
Memories, which mar my mentality.
My personality is molded from ashes.
It's wet with the rain of reality,
Making it a true struggle

5. Searching for Identity

To allow my heart to breathe
To sheathe my anger.

In my sanity am I truly sane?

No voices are in my head...check.
I can hold conversations, problem solve rationally...check.
Mind is not debased enough to commit a mass murder...
I comprehend pain,
Feel it in my veins, and accept change...check.
Then why do I adopt newfound ideas that are not my own,
Feed into those that are
Foreign to my beliefs.
The mainstream tells me to embrace immorality,
So, I tasted that lifestyle.
It tells me to live life lofty, and forget I have testosterone...
Be more feminine—with tight jeans your demeanor will scream swag,
So below your knees allow them to sag.
Then every new product produce, I need to buy, buy, buy.
Why am I this way
When I've seen what this does to people?
Why am I willing to try if I have the chance?

Am I truly sane in my insanity, comfortable in this so-called reality?

Or am I conscious, aware of what is real?

Nevertheless, this must all be,
Because I can touch it, smell it, taste it, see it, hear it all...
But it is all a day shower, fading away.
A mist with light revealing the hidden, it all has no substance.
So mirror with my reflection, do you have the answer to my question...
Am I truly sane?
Living this life, wasting this gift, with vanity and programmed
ambition,
This is a life lived with a profit motive, pushing me to the mundane.
Tell me am I truly sane...?

Marvin Picerne

∽

None of the young have an iron-clasp grip on their identities. But some, to be frank, *most* are beyond lost in who they are. Lost in wanting, they surrender the choice to follow the paths that uncover the truth of who they are as individuals, instead pacing through the pandemonium of confusion and misconception. And as seen in the poem above, society is more often than not the negative influence that forces us from ourselves, into a pattern of self-degradation and unoriginality. Popularity, corrupted by society, forces us from ourselves, transfiguring us into sheep–humanistic robots expected to abide by trends and adopt false personas for the mere purpose of gaining approval. Yet, is the benefit of an easier life worth the cost of losing our individuality?

In the following story, a girl with a short-circuited identity tries to find herself by associating with a highly-esteemed group of teenage elite. She hopes that if she can become a part of this exclusive society, her mislaid identity can return, giving her a lasting sense of worth and significance.

~

Grayson's Dimension

PROLOGUE

From dealing with death, I know that when desire goes unfulfilled, your very soul decays. Charred and corroded, you burn, consumed by conflicting senses of self–a jaded counterpart–a stranger with your face. Before the accident, I never considered that the dimensions of reality and surreality are parallel, that what I needed wasn't what I wanted.

Only when I was basking in the headlights, on the verge of death, did I see myself for the first time. Strung between dimensions, I glimpsed what I thought was Heaven. But I never had to look that far.

The sky burned, grey green in hue, a precedent to the coming rain. Pale, translucent streaks licked our moon-burned skin as we sat huddled together like baby sea turtles on the ghostly, rain-splattered beach. I shivered in spite of myself.

Stefon was listening to the Chicago soundtrack; I could hear "Nowadays" bellowing through his headphones. On my right, Zoey snored, ignorant to everything, like the ocean that met the skyline at the foot of the hill we rested on.

Then I spotted *them*, a golden mass of people, arisen like sunlight on the far side of the beach.

"Time to go," I announced to my friends, standing abruptly.

Stefon unplugged his earphones. I gave Zoey a shove and she awoke with a snort. The hideous yellow fedora she wore slid over her eyes as they snapped open.

"Hey, hey," she grumbled, "What gives?"

"The rain."

The rain was a scapegoat, a transparent excuse. It was *them* I wished to flee.

Zoey frowned. "The rain is lovely, Grayson."

"Speaking of lovely," Stefon coughed, "Check it out."

I did, and then immediately wished I hadn't. Evan Harper led the golden people, The Empire, across the vacant beach. The sky glowed green with envy. Alarmingly near external perfection, they strode, radiating joy and confidence. They had reason to hold high spirits. They entitled themselves the Empire because they made up the region's high school elite. Only the brightest, the most beautiful, and the most creative of people were accepted into this exclusive assembly.

Hot, swooping desire erupted like heart burn in my throat as I watched them slowly shrink into the distance, off to an unknown locale. No one knew what when on at their alleged meetings. Some called the Empire artists of performance, an undercover circus. Others declared them a satanic cult who executed bizarre, gory rituals, in which they sacrificed animals and inflicted their bodies with self-harm. Some people even went so far as to claim them inhuman. As for me, I believed them to be deliverance from my internal decay. In them, I would find what for years I had sought without avail— my identity. Evan—their leader—and The Empire swam, a mirage in my feverish gaze.

"For God's sake, wipe that drool off your lip," Zoey snickered, eyes flashing to the sky.

"Which one of us are you talking to?" Stefon inquired, dazed.

"Both of you. Your infatuation with The Empire, with *Evan*, is appalling."

"What's appalling is your lack of said infatuation."

Zoey shot an only mildly interested glance their way.

"I see tanning oil and teenage narcissism. How spectacular."

"No," I said, shaking my head, "They're more than that. I know they're special. I wish I could see them as they are, what they do when they are at their meetings."

Zoey laughed. "Why don't you go grovel at their feet and implore to be their groupie then?"

I leaned over and yanked the atrocious fedora off her bright blue head, tossing it into wind.

"Damn you, Grayson!" she yelled, stumbling down the hill to pursue the spiraling flash of yellow. I turned to Stefon, eyes flickering to his wrists. He swiftly folded his arms.

"How are you?" I asked.

"I'm not dead."

"Aside from the evident."

He slipped his iPod into his back jean pocket, quiet.

"Answer me."

"I'm a living Hell. But I am living. Because of you."

"No, not me. It isn't about me. It's you, Stef."

He smoothed his copper hair down with meticulous fingers.

"Stef, you're brilliant. You have to know you are. Promise that you'll never terrify me like that again. Promise me that you will be stronger."

"I can't promise that."

"And why not?" I demanded.

"Because I respect you too much to lie to you."

My glare burned a hole in his pupils. He smiled softly.

"But I promise I'll try."

I released a shaky breath, squeezing his hand. Zoey emerged from below the sandy dune.

"Are we okay?" she asked, glancing between us.

"Someday we will be," I replied, linking my arm through hers.

We ascended the hill and then walked to our bikes, which were parked on the edge of the curb; we mounted. Off we rode, the freaks, the misread and the disconnected, into the cold Florida rain. I squinted into the icy pellets, struggling for vision. My bike bounced over the elevations and dips in the uneven sidewalk. I winced as the handlebars dug into my ribcage. Ahead of me, Stefon and Zoey shimmered, colored patches in the grey. I pedaled faster, glancing right, cutting swiftly across the vacant, two-lane street.

As I was crossing, a scarlet van leapt out of the grey and the breath smashed out of my chest. I swerved my handlebars violently, electrocuted with terror, vision static. The van wailed, headlights blinding, and veered off sharply, clipping my back wheel. With a massive lurch, the bike hurtled to the pavement, taking me with it. I fell over myself, tumbling, breathless into the other lane of the street. Finally, I caught my body. I heard them screaming, the two who loved me. Relief flooded into my limbs, suffusing them with feeling. Slowly, shakily, I arose.

"It's okay," I said, voice cracking into relieved laughter, "I'm okay."

The sound was surreally loud. I wheeled around, flabbergasted. Two white-hot headlights engulfed me. The eighteen-wheeler lunged. I shielded my eyes from the light.

From above, I observed a girl lying on a hospital bed. Her skin was too white. Her auburn hair was tangled around her unconscious countenance. A stocky girl with dyed blue hair and a yellow hat sat hunched in a chair by the girl's side, silent. A boy with wire-rim glasses and a sweep of penny-colored hair stood at the foot of the bed, sobbing. The girl's mother watched from a corner, expression vacant. The girl's father indulged in work, his greatest love, at some far-off office, oblivious to her coma.

With a shallow gasp, I awoke, head throbbing. Black, neon paint-splattered walls, a shelf overflowing with books on travel, an easel poised vigilantly by the window...my room. A few items were different, however. The posters on the walls had altered. Dark, baleful photographs displaying rock bands like AC/DC and Nirvana were replaced with pictures of more current, radio pop artists.

The members of a band I didn't recognize grinned at me from above my door and I frowned back, only recognizing them from the lead singer, who starred in some reality show that I had only ever seen commercials of. The photographs above my bed, also, weren't what they were before. The first picture I noticed bewildered me. In it, my photographed self stood laughing, jubilant, in the arms of none other than Evan Harper. The next picture displayed me, wedged in between seven other girls, all of whom were tan, beautiful, and practically oozing mystery. *The Empire.*

I involuntarily clutched at my throat, ruled by horror. Memory of the accident struck me into incredulity. This, this world right here, wasn't reality. I was imprisoned in a vivid dream, or a Heaven of some kind? A violent tremble shook my chest and I untangled my body from my sheets, which were damp with sweat. Had I died? Through the window, a sinking scarlet sun winked at me as it slipped behind the scraggly tree-line. It looked uncannily like the real sun—the one I once knew. My face fell into my hands.

A knock sounded on my door.

"Come in," I called, believing it to be my mother. *My alternate mother.* How could I deal with her right now?

The door swung in and my fake father stepped into my fake room. I took a step back.

"Hello, Daddy."

"Hi, Baby," he greeted, beaming at me.

My throat tightened. *Baby?*

"I just wanted to tell you that Evan called. He said he's going to pick you up in an hour."

"Oh—okay. Yeah. Right, yeah."

"Alright, Sweetie."

I stared at him and helpless tears sprung to my eyes. Concern etched his clean-shaven face. Concern for *me.*

"Gracie, what's wrong?"

"N-nothing, Daddy. Not wrong. Right."

Unable to resist the urge, I ran to him, throwing my arms around his neck. He enveloped me in his embrace, pulling my body into him. My chest shook in silent, tearless sobs.

"Baby, I don't know why you're upset, but whatever it is, I'm here for you. I love you, Gracie."

I melted at the words, their beautiful unfamiliarity. I even forgot Evan's name. My words rolled, warbled, through my lips.

"I do, too..." I swallowed, "love you, I mean. I always have, Daddy."

The wind blow-dried my hair and warmed me to the point of trembling. Evan flashed his perfect teeth at me from the driver's seat of the corvette and jet-black and it nearly caused me heartburn. Exhilaration vibrated inside me, like a drug-induced haze. The corvette whipped around a corner with alacrity, tearing into a parking space too quickly, causing the car to bump the parking block with a jolt.

"Sorry 'bout that, Babe," Evan laughed, jumping out and helping me climb over the car door. I took his hand. It was damp and burning.

I stared up at him, shivering with attraction and feverishly anticipating what was to come. When Evan arrived on my doorstep, after animatedly greeting me and my parents and saying that I looked beautiful, he told me that we were going to a meeting—with the Empire. Now, I was speechless with excitement; my zeal diminished the preexisting pangs of fear and doubt I felt toward this new dimension. I know that I should have been dubious of everything, but ever since I saw the love—for me—on my father's face, I became totally opposed to doubt. I desperately wanted to believe that this world was real, because it was everything I had wanted.

Still, I deeply wished that Stefon and Zoey were here, to share this otherwordly experience with me. Once the secret of the Empire was revealed to us, unshielded from the mystique, Stefon would stomp his depression into the dust and Zoey would admit she was wrong in ever doubting their relevance. And when I told my friends about what had happened between my father and I, they would cry for me. Or maybe they wouldn't–my father's affection toward me wasn't a peculiar occurrence in this dimension. Before Evan and I left the house, I called them several times, but neither of my friends answered their phones. I made myself concentrate on Evan, my unrequited crush for the past four years, and promised to fill Stefon and Zoey in on everything afterwards.

As soon as we began walking down the boardwalk that led to the beach, I started to hear a beat, toxic and throbbing. My heart hammered as Evan slid his hand into mine, swinging our arms back and forth with the erotic rhythm of the pulsing music. I couldn't fathom what was coming. So long I had spent in anguished longing over this group. What I was convinced I'd never be a part of (in italics), I thought, smiling wryly.

How much time I spent soring my mind to conceive an idea of what possibly could occur where the rest of the world couldn't see the Empire, where they unleashed their creativity and beauty. I was always on the outside, always unconnected from others and myself, but no more. Stefon and Zoey and I could all be a part of something extraordinary, something that held more gravity than just the three of us. So many mindless rumors were launched by mindless mouths around school—who the Empire were, what they stood for, what they were involved in, and I, Grayson—the lonely artist, the dreamer—was about to uncover the secret that so many wanted to know. Evan and I, hand in hand, rounded the corner, stepping onto the sand.

The black sky smoked from the great bonfire that illuminated the vast party. As Evan and I approached the mass of swaying bodies, yells and cheers began to reverberate around the crowded beach, until everyone was lifting red cups into the air, an unholy toast. I took a couple steps backward in utter shock, but Evan tugged me along by the hand. All of a sudden I was engulfed on all sides by sweaty golden bodies.

Girls I didn't know were kissing my cheeks, leaving smudges of salmon pink, crimson, and lavender all over my face. A few guys kissed me too, leaving the scent of alcohol and smoke hanging wispily around me, clouding my head. One guy's mouth came so close to mine that his tongue brushed the corner of my upper lip. I stood, frozen, feet cemented to the ground. My hazy gaze leapt to Evan, anticipating disapproval at this inappropriate display, but he just laughed, playfully smacking the creep upside the head.

The Empire eventually then returned to the bonfire, leaving Evan and I on the outskirts of the party, where a few couples were rolling in the sand, limbs frantically grabbing and wanting. I fixed my gaze on Evan; the firelight gleamed in his hazel eyes and his skin burned so, seeming to be ignited from the inside. I looked down at our intertwined fingers.

My hand was obscenely white compared to his. Evan grinned, saying he was going to find us a couple drinks. I nodded. The party, the alcohol, the dancing...all an absolute surprise to me. But once the party settled down...then I would witness what the Elite spoke of at school in hushed voices—the beauty and amazement that set them apart, that made them special. It would occur and I would see it with my own eyes. This wasn't it; I wouldn't accept that. I knew there was more to this group, to Evan, than that. Most teenagers partied, anyway. I could wait for the relevance to settle in. I would wait. While Evan was gone, I vigorously scrubbed my lipsticked cheeks with my knuckles, fearing infection.

Evan returned with two red cups, handing one to me. I hesitated. He gave me a questioning stare. I reluctantly took a sip and was rueful. I swallowed with difficulty and the alcohol scorched my throat, stronger than anything I'd ever tasted. I might as well have guzzled gasoline. I poured the rest of the cup in the sand, while Evan was engaged in conversation with some buzzed friend of his.

Confusion and distress overwhelmed me. Everyone was hurtling toward the state of being absolutely wasted. What *is* this? Evan talked to the guy for several minutes about sports and some concert, possessively clasping my hand in his the entire time. He turned to face me after the conversation had ended, asking me if I wanted to dance. I swallowed, beyond lost in everything.

"Is this—" I swallowed hard, tasting leftover vodka. "Is this... all it is? What—what is our purpose? What do we do?"

Evan frowned for a second, forehead furrowing, and then he laughed.

"Do? What do you mean? This...this is what we do at its best."

He gestured to the people, dancing sordidly around us, and I felt nauseated.

"Oh...oh no," I murmured, eyes suddenly very blurry.

Ignorant to my distress, Evan grinned and pulled me into the midst of the dancing bodies.

"Come on, Babe. Let's dance."

Brokenly, I followed him. I didn't know what else to do. At least he still was good, a glowing soul amidst the immorality and the superficiality. Maybe he could be.

Surrounding the blaze, bodies grinded against each other. My skin was aglaze in sweat. Up close, the Empire weren't as unique and physically immaculate as Stefon and I had made them out to be as we watched from afar. The girls bore all but a few choice inches of skin; their makeup gleamed on their skin, thickly caked on, and their hair beamed, conspicuously bleached. The guys yelled drunkenly, on the verge of being wholly obnoxious, smelling distinctly of sweat. Evan smelled good, however, like musty cologne. As we danced, I felt my body lightening, my limbs loosening, until the pulsating beat lifted me into hazy elation.

Forget the nothingness of this place, of these people, because Evan was always real–the only one here who ever showed any kindness to me in my old life, the brilliance within the bad. He was always good, always real.

"You're beautiful, Grayson," Evan murmured, pressing closer to me.

I couldn't reply, too breathless from the dance, from the moment. The foreign words rung for a lapse of time; finally I could hear the music again. I tried to disregard the fact that the prevalence of the Empire had been nothing but illusion; I tried to disregard the fact that Evan was president of such a group. He cupped my hips with his large, golden hands. I let myself see the cool black of my eyelids. Then I felt fingers slide beneath my top. I froze. The hand caressed me, a filthy betrayal. I saw him again and he smiled, leaning in to whisper something in my ear. I felt sickened, shocked; he was my very own stranger. His hand curved around the underside of my breast and I jerked away, disgusted—not by him, but by myself.

Evan grinned drunkenly. "What's wrong, Babe?"

"Don't call me 'Babe'," I spat, stumbling over a couple of discarded red cups as I backed away from him. The smoke saturated my lungs and burned tears out of my eyes.

Evan frowned crookedly.

"What the hell is the matter with you, Grayson ? Stop being such a tight-ass bitch."

I didn't answer. Instead, I turned and sprinted away from the repulsive scene. The hill felt steeper than it should have been. When I reached the top, I was out of breath, but the smoke had cleared from my head and the music was nothing more than a subtle beat. I knew what I needed. But I didn't know how to find it, lost too far into a never-ending dream that had suddenly become reality. Everything I had desired in my last life was a lie; I had been sophmoric, ignorant, moronic, drunk by what I thought I wanted.

I saw a boy, about sixteen, throwing up behind the bike rack in the parking lot. I waited for him to finish and then approached him, asking shakily for the date. Quizzically, he responded that it was the thirteenth, stating what I'd already instinctively known.

The day after my accident. I consulted my phone. It wasn't too late. Tonight, the play that Stefon starred in premiered at the De Le Carte Theatre, an event that, had I been in my home dimension, would have been the highlight of my month. I ran my fingertips over the cold metal of the bike racks. One bike wasn't locked to the rack, and I seized it, ignoring my moral whims. Tonight, rules were irrelevant. On the road, I watched for cars this time.

After ten minutes or so had elapsed, the modest little brick theatre lunged out of the night. I dismounted the bike, propping it against the side of the building, next to the entrance. I opened the heavy mahogany wooden door and slipped unnoticed as a spirit down the dimly-lit hallway. The corridor opened into a small lobby; I purchased a ticket with a few crumbled bills I'd luckily left in the pocket of my jean shorts, grateful for that as well as the fact that the lobbyist allowed late entry. I quietly entered.

Haunting music filled my ears, eloquent and rich compared to the lustful throbs that my eardrums had previously endured. I glanced forward. Stefon was not currently onstage. I scanned the crowd, spotted Zoey, and hurried to her, sliding into the empty seat beside hers.

"Hey," I murmured.

She blinked. "Um, hello."

The blatant truth dawned upon me, a horrific revelation. I wasn't friends with Zoey and Stef in this reality. My nausea returned, overwhelming me.

"H-hi," I stammered, "I'm Grayson."

"I know who you are." Zoey looked away. "You and your boyfriend lead the Empire, group of exclusion. Am I right?"

"Yes. I suppose you are," I said, slowly.

"So why are you here?"

I stared at the stage, searching. "I came to see Stefon."

Zoey seized my wrist fiercely, suddenly, her eyes glazing over in obvious agony.

"You heartless bitch," she whispered, tone quavering, "Stefon died less than a month ago."

My surreal, dilapidated dimension shuttered, then fell to pieces.

"That's not possible!" I cried.

Astounded silence momentarily suffocated the theater. It seemed every head turned to stare at me. Only the actors onstage hadn't frozen, professionally resilient to the crazy audience outcry. I could care less of what everyone thought of me. Nothing mattered but the loss of my best friend and the cavity inside me where he once resided. Nothing mattered but the flawed reality that I'd give everything here to return to. A hundred eyes stared, but didn't see me. Yet for the first time in years, I did.

"I think you should go now," Zoey said, quietly. She seemed uneasy.

She was right. I belonged here with her as much as I belonged with Evan and his Empire. I left the De Le Carte Theatre, shaken to the core.

It was cold for a Florida summer night and darker than I had remembered. I heard the rumble of cars on the highway. The line between surreal and real was too thin, like a spider web. If I touched it, would it disintegrate? If you die in a dream, you wake up in reality. I will destroy this web.

Stefon had done what I had convinced him out of in reality. Terrible tears that I had managed to restrain the entire night seared like soap in my eyes. I had lost myself to desire. Stefon was gone. He and Zoey were my everything. My infatuation with the Empire had been moronic, a plastic lie. My friends were raw, flawed beauty.

This dimension is an adulated illusion. And I'm a fool.

Only one thing remains to do.

I left the bike waiting besides the building, and I started running toward the highway lights. I could barely see through the veil of my tears. For the first time tonight, all felt surreal. I ran until my chest hurt and my legs were throbbing dully. If I emerged from this alive, I resolved to start working out more.

I reached the exit ramp that fed into the massive highway, Interstate 4. My clumsy feet stumbled along the side of the road, along the lopsided grassy knoll, where plastic bags and flickers of paper whisked around my legs. Cars roared by me so fast that terror left me momentarily paralyzed. Still, I kept running until I had reached the top of the ramp and was standing on the side of I-4. The din was indescribable; the speed made me shiver.

If my death in this dimension were akin to my near-death in my old dimension, would I return? Did I have even a chance of survival? What of the person in the other car–the one that would hit the girl. What would become of them?

A pang struck me out of nowhere. What about my father? I swallowed. To lose his love...but no. It was all part of the illusion.

Only when I was basking in the headlights, on the verge of death, did I see myself for the first time. Strung between dimensions, I glimpsed what I thought was Heaven. But, ironically, I never had to look that far.

I didn't fear, because I didn't think. Eyes screwed shut, throwing a prayer to the sky, I strode into the light.

From above, I observed a girl lying on a hospital bed. Her skin was too white. Her auburn hair was tangled around her unconscious countenance. Three pairs of weary eyes stared at her as she slept. Then the monitor changed, determining her fate.

THE END

SMB

Popularity isn't what it seems. The outsiders aren't the only ones under an illusion. We think that the achievement of popularity is ultimate, but in actuality, it is a step down for each individual. The people who are popular, who condemn and ignore you, are even more confounded, utterly deceived by the did I see myself for the first time. Popularity may be a label, but it isn't a name—it isn't an identity. Popularity proves to be individuality's inverse, smiting identity because it forces you into a character that isn't your own; it's an interminable acting job. How can you "be yourself," discover yourself and others for what they are, when you define your prevalence by your popularity? What I've learned, from experiencing how that crowd compresses their character to the degree that they do, is that this is essentially impossible.

I acknowledge that obtaining popularity establishes pride and self-confidence that has potential to lead to growth. But this confidence is almost always false and this pride can be on the brink of excessive, and therefore, toxic. If you have any respect for your individuality, your uniqueness, then give popularity the cold-shoulder. Popularity taints good people, and popular people devastate real people.

You can't trust people who live falsely, merely for themselves, not to attempt to annihilate your eccentricity, your individualism; you must combat them—without cruelty—to defend yourself against those who attempt to bleed out your weird, render you normal. You have to be able to trust yourself not to conform into the conventionality. Step away from the norm and into the oddity. That's where you will find yourself.

6. To Sacrifice Who You Are

*"To be yourself in a world that is constantly trying to make
you something else is the greatest accomplishment."*
Ralph Waldo Emerson

You have to be perfect

Perfection's required
If you want to fit in.
A certain weight you must be–
No greater than thin.

Your skin must be fair,
Nothing can mar.
This means no pimples,
This means no scars.

You can't be a nerd,
No, don't work hard in school.
To ace any test
Is considered uncool.

You must own trendy clothes,
Must blow lots of money.
And to be one season late
Is to be thought of as funny.

You have to be outgoing,
You cannot be shy.
You have to be strong,
You can never cry.

Why do you have to be someone you're not?
Why can't you just be yourself,
Quirky traits and all,
Instead of a forgotten book on the shelf?

Sarah

What is Popularity In Itself?

It is–
Being liked by the majority.
Being known by a lot of people.
Being normal.

But Sometimes Popularity is:

Mistreating others.
Abandoning your old friends for not being "cool enough"–
Having fake friends.
Striving to be what is considered popular
By not being yourself...
Just because yourself *isn't considered cool.*

Tiana Barfield

∿

When I was in middle school, I sought after popularity. For years I had tired of being on the outside, mocked and bullied for both my appearance and character, and thought that if I could be accepted by others, then I could find the strength to discard my self-loathing and accept myself. More than anything, I wanted to yank myself out of the haze of teenage confusion and uncover who was beneath the barrier of my external appearance. I thought popularity would do this for me. But maybe I'm overestimating myself—maybe I just wanted my misery to end.

So, arrogantly determined, I pushed myself out of my comfort zone (a positive action) to attempt to befriend the people of the popular clique at my school (a less than positive action). Finally, after copious unsuccessful stabs at acceptance, I developed what I believed was a friendship with one of the core popular girls.

Initially, I was utterly pleased at my accomplishment. This, after all, was what I had desired for years since the beginning of my downfall, my isolation—a chance to prove myself worthy enough to associate with the social front-runners of my school.

However, the truth of what I had blindly stumbled into soon struck me forcefully, popping the glitzy bubble of illusion that had such a short time before dazzled me. Either my naivety had been been vast, or I'd simply refused to believe what deep down I had known all along.

These girls could be vindictive and cruel beyond their years. They not only made horrendous comments about the physical appearance and lifestyles of the people less socially adapted than them, but the minute one girl in the circle wasn't present, they immediately criticized her as well. They tossed out malicious, biting little insults at one another for the mere, sadistic purpose of tearing one another down, and committed brutal acts of betrayal to one another such as setting each other up for mortifying situations and trying to become involved with one another's boyfriends.

These girls were almost comically shallow; the matters which they consistently discussed and were concerned over were ludicrously superficial, and I realized I held no likeness to them in matters of interests. I wasn't an idiot, though I had been a fool; I began slowly relinquishing my ties from the group, once again seeking to mend my old friendships—the ones of value. Even so, the false kindness and charisma of the popular clique ambushed my naivety, allowing them to keep snatching me back into their circle. Their deceptively charming personas began to overwhelm me, rubbing off on me.

I grew shallow and uncharacteristically irritable. My passion for my previous concerns faltered, deferred, to the point that it became easily perceptible to my family and few real friends at the time that I had changed. They warned me about my new friendship, and I, guileless and under the illusion of ignorance, did not heed their warnings.

I suffered the consequences for my actions when I made the mistake of telling the popular girl I'd initially befriended the name of the boy I was, at the time, desperately in love with (at least as desperately in love as you can be at age thirteen). She smiled in something like amusement when I told her. I wasn't one to like someone based on his appearance or confidence, but on his character.

For the entire year, I had been preoccupied with this boy, admiring him deeply because I found him compassionate, funny, and genuine. Merely days after I told her, I discovered that my so-called friend was involved with him. At the time, it was irrelevant to me that their relationship lasted the mere span of two weeks. What mattered to me was that I had been betrayed, and my illusion had been brutally shattered.

I had lost the better qualities of myself to a venomous association and had developed incredibly negative traits to replace my more pleasant ones. Feeling moronic and like I'd deserved what I'd gotten, I abandoned the "friendship" and set out to discover real ones. That proved to be one of the best decisions I have yet made.

Luckily for me, I wasn't immersed in this world before I realized that these people were demoralizing me and turning me into someone I wasn't and who I honestly would never want to be. Not only that, but perceptively, their treatment of me–of anyone, really–didn't bode well for their character. For other people, however, adjourning from the over-embellished popular mystique is not so easy.

It's fortunate if you manage to avoid close association with people who will tear you down and change you for the worse, but most aren't that lucky. While some people are merely friends with the wrong people, others are entangled in negative family situations, blood relatives who are verbally or physically abusive verses affectionate and accepting. The best thing for every person is straightforward and palpable, but not unproblematic. If you aren't with people who encourage you to be the extreme of the zaniest, oddest, and most interesting parts about you, then to be wholly satisfied and to be happy will be a difficult task.

But while you do need to find these type of people (especially if, for any reason, you are forced to be in company with those who aren't a positive influence on who you are as a person), you never will be able until you first learn to accept the exceptionality, the bizarreness, of yourself. You may not always have that friend, that group, but you'll always be in your own company, and if you don't learn to respect yourself and have confidence in who you are, then no one else can either.

So simple it is—respect your uniqueness and stand up for others who may also be harassed for exhibiting this realness that disturbs the more intolerant of people. In the one act play below, this strength and confidence in self is compellingly displayed.

⁓

Populars Versus Hoi Polloi

I ACT PLAY

By: *Tanquesha Mills*

Characters:

Nycole Lovelane: the most popular girl in Greenville High, leader of the popular clique; she gives everyone the impression that she has high self-esteem and undiluted pride.

Tanquesha: the new girl in school; she is good-hearted, strong, and confident in who she is.

Ida: a follower

Principal Coleman: the stern, no-nonsense principal of Greenville High

Setting: Greenville, SC
Time: present day

Scene i.

(Tanquesha strolls down the halls of Greenville High. Even though she's new and quite shy, she holds her head high, smiling and greeting the people that walk past her. Out of nowhere comes a clique of girls. The clique leader gruffly bumps Tanquesha as she walks by, sending the new girl's books flying to the floor.)

Tanquesha *(with a questioning gesture, slightly angry)*: What the—

Nycole *(nastily, with a condescending smile):* FYI, I'm the one around here who sets the standards for people like you. You could say that this is my territory. Feel free to make yourself comfortable *(threatening)*...but when you make yourself too comfortable, that's when I may have a problem with you.

(She dramatically turns and strides away. Her friends follow, each one giving Tanquesha a vicious scowl as they pass.)

Tanquesha *(angrily mumbles, stooping to pick up her books)*: Stupid, trifling, snobs...

Ida *(approaches Tanquesha)*: Hi—I'm Ida. *(She assists Tanquesha and then extends her hand)*

Tanquesha *(shaking her hand)*: Hey, I'm Tanquesha.

Ida: Nice to meet you. So you're new here?

Tanquesha: Yeah. What *is* that girl's problem? *(Thumbing toward Nycole, who is chatting with her clique across the hallway)*

Ida *(simply)*: Nycole Lovelane isn't *only* the most popular and richest girl at Greenville High; she also has the bitchiest attitude.

Tanquesha *(rolling her eyes, exasperated)*: Populars...they think they're the stuff.

Ida *(mildly shocked)*: And why *shouldn't* they? *(dreamily)* They may be arrogant, but they're beautiful, rich, athletic...

Tanquesha *(plainly)*: Since when are those the standards of being a good person? They're just people. There are many *hoi* *polloi*—"normal people" *(air quotes)*— who are those things too, you know. *(Loudly)* What's so special about *them*? They're just a bunch of stuck-up nobodies, because that's how they treat other people. They use *(again air quotes)* "normal people" as pawns in their vapid, self-indulged worlds, just to make them feel better about themselves.

(Nycole and her crew hear Tanquesha and turn to glare at her)

Ida *(shy, nervously)*: Please lower your voice.

Tanquesha *(even louder)*: Forget them *(looking directly at the popular clique and addressing them)*. *I* have just as much of a right to be here as *you* do! You may have the best looks, the most guys, or whatever the hell else people worship you for, but you're all *nobodies*...because what you are is a reflection of how you treat people. *(under her breath, but audibly)* You low-down whores.

(The girls advance toward Tanquesha fiercely. Ida hovers, frightened, behind her. Tanquesha stands her ground firmly, more annoyed than anything else, and certainly not afraid of the threat.)

Tanquesha (boldly): Bring it on.

(The popular girls come to an abrupt halt in front of her.)

Tanquesha: *(still holding her position, smirking)*: Yeah, that's what I thought.

(Principal Coleman enters.)

Principal Coleman *(stern voice)*: What's going on in here? Someone complained of a disturbance obstructing the hallway.

(Tanquesha turns around in surprise at the Principal's arrival. She and the popular girls are indeed blocking the hallway. Ida slowly slips away into the background with the crowd.)

Nycole *(puts her hands on her hips, tilting her chin up in her superior stance)*: Principal Coleman, this new girl was screaming through the hall like a psycho case and called us all whores.

Principal Coleman: *(folds her arms and raises an eyebrow at Tanquesha)*: Is this true, young lady?

Tanquesha: Misleadingly true, Ma'am. Only after she knocked my books out of my hands and threatened me did I do such a thing...

(Principal Coleman gives Nycole a questioning frown.)

Nycole *(jerks and gasps as if she was slapped in the face)*: I. Did. Not!

Principal Coleman: Mhm. A likely story. You two girls go straight to my office.

Scene ii.

(The two girls wait in the principal's spacious, plush office. There are file cabinets and a waxed, mahogany desk in the room, and the girls sit in maroon chairs with velvet cushions. Principal Coleman's walls are covered with certificates, thank you notes, medals, and awards.)

Nycole *(giving Tanquesha the evil eye)*: This is all your fault. You had to show up—with your picture perfect, cordial smile, stealing attention from me!

Tanquesha *(laughs, appalled at her reason for anger)*: Are you jealous?

Nycole *(furiously)* Don't make fun of me!

Tanquesha *(seriously)*: Nycole, if looks are what you're so concerned about...you're pretty, prettier than me.

Nycole *(crying)*: I know *that*.

Tanquesha: *(raises her eyebrows at Nycole's comment)* I don't get why you're so upset. I also don't get why populars feel so compelled to be so arrogant and mean. Look, I'm sorry I called you a whore. But we're all people, and most of the other students see you all as gods for some obscure reason. Sure you may be pretty, athletic, rich, sly, cunning, and so on, but in the end, we're *all* the same thing—human beings.

Nycole *(sniffles, wiping away tears)*: You *normals* just don't know how to use what you have to your advantage. You wait to be noticed rather than put yourselves out there, like we do. You try to act innocently instead of being daring. You are always thinking and calculating instead of just *doing*. You all get to just be yourselves while we have to set examples for others, show them how to be cool. We have to be perfect while you all—you all use your imperfection as *weirdness*. We can't live that *(air quotes)* "normal" life.

Tanquesha: Well, maybe so, but I think you all could be "normal" if you wanted to. What you consider the normal lifestyle is actually the real way to live. Your problem is that you let others pressure you into being some stereotype instead of being who you really want to be. You call us nobodies, but obviously we are the somebodies, because you all feel the need to impress *us* and make *us* feel either good or bad. If you really think about it, we are all in the same boat here.

Nycole *(scoffing, back to her arrogant self)*: We don't need to impress the likes of *you*!! We—

Tanquesha *(waving her off, exhausted by her incapability to understand)*: Girl, shut the hell up.

(Principal Coleman enters)

Principal Coleman: Well, let's get this over with, shall we?

THE END

~

In order to develop your personality, you don't want but need to be in the presence of people who will challenge you to be a better person. However, you must know the contrast between this and enduring the company of people who push you away from yourself, compromise your beliefs and ideals. To sacrifice who you are for the sole purpose of being popular is the absolute worst act that you can commit in regard to expressing yourself in a singular and distinctive way. It isn't worth it in the short or long run, and goes against yourself as an individual. You will later in life deeply regret that you fabricated a lifestyle for yourself merely to please other people.

However, you will never look back and truly regret being your weird, bizarre, amazing self and surrounding yourself with people who truly adore those strange parts of you.

And this is imperative. However, many personality types and many characteristics that should be highly regarded are instead mocked. Being rarer, more exceptional than what most have, they are deemed "weirdness."

People who are kind to everyone are usually ridiculed, taken advantage of. Is kindness weird now? People who aren't straight are condemned, criticized, for being honest with themselves and others about whom they love. So honesty is no longer a virtue?

People who aren't into current music or trends? They are claimed weird, unable to live in the now. People who pursue their studies with vigor, who are interested in science or reading or such? They are labled as nerds, unacceptable for being eager to escalate their intelligence. And God forbid you defy modern fashion, modern trends, and modern society. Some people in high school hate what they don't understand, are repelled by it. That's why they tag us with labels. After high school, however, weirdness is usually what makes a name for these people, what allows them to succeed in life.

Not all of this age condemn oddness. There are those people who will embrace the extremes of your character, who will take you to that place where you realize that you know yourself to such a greater extent than you ever thought you would.

They may not be the safe ones, the sure ones, or even the sane ones. They most likely will not be the popular ones. But they will be the real ones. And they will be the right ones.

7. The Real People— The Right Ones

"A friend is one that knows you as you are,
understands where you have been, accepts what you have
become, and still, gently allows you to grow."
William Shakespeare

"One's friends are that part of the human race with
which one can be human."
George Santayana

Be Who You Are—Jackie Wilstrup

Two years ago, if you had asked me who the hell I thought I was, I would have told you that I didn't know. I did not have my own identity. I was too afraid and ended up letting my fear hold back my true self. I took my personality, threw it in the shredder, and tried to be the person I thought others would like—the person that people would stare at with envy and wish they could be or at least be close to.

I had friends and I loved them, but I was so self-conscious that I didn't let myself truly live. They had no idea of the crazy, hilarious, insane, and happy person I was. All they saw was the sad and dejected teenager who lived and breathed music. Truth is the only reason I didn't kill myself that year was my music.

No matter how bad life got or how misunderstood or lost I felt, my music kept me alive, whether it was Rachmaninov, Versailles, or Lady GaGa. I'm still here because of those artists, and for that I am eternally grateful. It's amazing how someone cantillating about what tragedies they have been through can be so healing.

My family was of no help either. I come from a family who are all left-sided thinkers, meaning they are structured people. None of them could understand what was happening to me. It was a new experience for us. I was the first problem child, with my rejection of authority, my need to be right all the time, and my tendency to say horrible, awful things that you should never say to your parents. Needless to say the horrible feeling of guilt still eats away at my heart.

Last year though, everything became so different. I entered high school with the attitude that nothing would change, that I would continue this façade for the rest of my life, that life would always be dull and monochrome.

Then I met the "Table in the Shade," a group of interesting outsiders at my school, and life as I knew it changed. They showed me that I shouldn't care what those popular kids think because in five years they wouldn't matter, their opinions wouldn't matter. It opened my eyes and I began to see the world in a new kaleidoscopic way. Instead of everything being black and white, there were now rainbow hues shining on the world. Even in the darkest of places there was light, and I knew everything was going to be better. Everything *was* better, and now I'm a better person because of it.

My personality came back slowly, but I started to truly become myself again. To be yourself—it's amazing and it's something that everyone should strive for. Basically, what I'm trying to say is that it's so much more rewarding to embrace your personality and meet people who accept all of you.

∽

Human beings weren't meant to live in seclusion from others. Below is true story of a beautiful girl who never knew her potency and the difficulty she faced due to her distinctiveness.

∽

Mental torsion, warp me tangled.

The remnants of a heart eerily mangled
Beyond repair...
Her stare, like a paroxysm of lightning,
Stung the sky a violet hue.
She never knew
How she shone.
All she saw were the gargoyles,
Etched, banal and bantering,
Into her never-ending night.
They gouged out the wax of her flickering esteem,
A candle swallowed by
Callous vanity, by immoral dreams.
They were horrendous,
Unlike what they seemed.
She glowed, like the ocean
Of innumerous hues.
But she never knew.
All she saw was social regularity,
Herself an impaired rarity.
All she saw was the illusion of normalcy,
Herself a disheveled infrequency.
She believed the bizarre beautiful,
They scorched it at its roots.
She adored the non-ideal,

They strangled imperfection into submission.
The confusion of life's greatest illusion is that
It contradicts its prevalent statement—
Perfection should suffuse your life.
But hate morphs into passion in their eyes,
And truth is entangled with the crucial white lie.
Physical immorality is met with intercepted acceptance.
No longer are insensitivity and betrayal deemed as decadence.
So her heart bled anguish through her eyes.
Her being wracked from copious tries—
Stabs at perfection that are enveloped by soul.
With their sardonic stares,
She will never feel whole.
But the Vibrants deemed freaks
Salvaged her heart,
Dissipated the criticism that tore her apart,
Until her being seared with hope.
With fellow strange ones at her side,
She knows she can cope.

SMB

~

It is far from difficult to see where different teenagers fall on the pyramid of social acceptance. However, the popularity system is not always as stereotyped as you observe on television. I have met so-called nerds who are accepted by the popular clan, and for that reason view their intelligence as an elevation above the rest.

The football jock also isn't always society's star; a once-popular football player I heard of was completely shunned once the rumor that he was gay began to circulate. So no status guarantees acceptance and things are not always as one might assume, but you can almost always pin down anyone's status and reputation merely by observing the way that person walks, acts, and addresses others. That is most certainly not to say that you can stake someone's personality solely upon observation. But you can usually determine who's considered "important" or less so by merely witnessing them interact with others, *particularly* in a school environment.

If you're on the outside looking in, from experience and insight, you can usually distinguish what kind of people the popular people are. That's not to say that they are *always* the bad people, because that is certainly untrue and imprudent; some popular people are popular because they are genuinely open and friendly to everyone or because of similar reason, but I will boldly state that this is usually not the case. More often than not, the people who are exclusive are the people who exclude. To exclude is to deem someone less than you, less relevant to exist, more appropriate, to say, *die* before you would.

As dire as such an assumption may seem, am I wrong to make it? That is what exclusive people feel either on the surface or further down beneath. Either that or they are incredibly ignorant in the way that they regard their lifestyle and their social standing.

These people usually don't deserve the recognition and accolades that they receive in such abundance; they are smitten with it most occasionally because of some minor quirks they possess or because of someone who's already popular they happen to be associated with. It doesn't need to be stated that the glory of the popular people is severely hyperbolic. These people in most cases did little to nothing to prove themselves superior to the rest; usually the traits that instigated their burst of recognition are excessive pride, shallow vanity, corrosive confidence, or all of the above. Certainly not reasons to be worshipped or admired so, but they, more often than not, *are*.

So when you are on the outside, perceiving these things, abandon the longing and the hurt, because you are worth so much more than someone who wears a mask for a face. To do this on your own, even if you have some semblense of security in who you are, is exceedingly difficult and saddening to do alone. You need people like you, real people, who aren't manipulative and artificial, who accept you completely—not just in your ideal, most airbrushed state—but at your worst and when you least want to be yourself.

For every real person in this world, it's a different friend or few friends who heals the scars of pains they thought they'd never stop feeling and enhances their lives to the point that they once again can enjoy life verses simply trying to survive it. Any friend or group of friends is wonderful to find solace and relationship in as long as they love you as yourself, are loyal to you, and are genuine.

The real people are always the right ones. The fake people, honest to God, are nearly always clandestinely envious of what is real and what is special. Most of them lash out at or burn by silence those people for this reason alone. Due to their shallowness and obliviousness to what they should strive to be, theythey are not in position or state of heart to achieve your level of realness, of trueness, and inside, that makes them (either consciously or subconsciously) ache.

Until I formed friendships with the people who were were sincere and strange, I was utterly miserable. Every concrete belief, every erratic thought, and every profound desire I had that I couldn't share with anyone else haunted me, becoming another brick that sealed me off from the world I felt I held no kinship to. At that point, only my music understood me. I decided that I needed therapy, because if what I felt was so bizarre to the point that no one else could relate to it, then I must be deranged on some level.

Nothing but *that* idea was wrong with me, but I never knew it until I met the right people, the people who I am close friends with today. Now when I voice something aloud that is preoccupying me or plaguing my mind, I receive in return, "That's not strange. I feel like that all the time," instead of shocked, mildly disturbed expressions and a change of conversation.

The way to decipher if someone is real, although circumstantially difficult, can be seen in the way they treat the people around them and the way they seem to perceive themselves. There isn't a list of qualities to look for to distinguish someone as "real" or "fake." There also aren't two categories into which all people are contained; all people are, to some extent, a mixture of the two.

What percentage you are real and artificial is irrelevant; what's important is which one you strive to be. And a person being upright about who they are does not automatically classify them as being *real*. Being real means genuinely trying to be a good person and honestly displaying traits or qualities of oneself that make you characteristically different or unique from the next person. You naturally won't find solace until you find the people who are real enough to be real with you.

The presence of these real people, these true friends, is so extraordinary, so revolutionary, that words cannot describe its pertinence. Never have I been happier than I am when I'm in the presence of those people who I am so intensely, emotionally connected with.

One girl who is now my best friend opened up to me years ago, showing me kindness when I was a stranger in a new place and no one else dared to. Another very close friend has more than once saved my life when I am at my absolute lowest, suffering with self-confidence or a broken heart. When I was still partially a child, a friend I no longer know showed me how to be an individual when everyone else didn't understand why I sought after what was outside the norm. One close friend of mine has always been there, even when my others have showed me dissatisfaction or disdain. But what all my friends do is love me, comprehend me, and save me every single day. Cliched or not, it is what I know to be truth.

Nonetheless, finding friendship with the right, real people does not ensure perfection, or anything close to it. Everyone will wound you at one point or another. We all irreversibly screw one another up, for better or for worse. You have to decide for yourself which ones are worth suffering for. But what the real people will do right is love you as you are, and they won't wish anything less than the best on you, ever. That is what is guaranteed in loving—and being loved—by the right ones.

8. The Beauty of Bizarre (And the Nothing of Normalcy)

"There are people who are generic. They make generic responses and they expect generic answers. They live inside a box and they think people who don't fit into their box are weird. But I'll tell you what, generic people are the weird people. They are like genetically-manipulated plants growing inside a laboratory, like indistinguishable faces, like droids. Like ignorance."
C. JoyBell C.

Strangeness is a necessary ingredient in beauty.
Charles Baudelaire

I once held the belief that beauty was defined by the measure of closeness that one could achieve to perfection. When I heard the word *beautiful*, my mind immediately flashed to an image of a frighteningly symmetrical man or woman, airbrushed in magazine form, physically appearing to be perfect, and, at the time unknown to me, utterly artificial. However, the more I've grown through those wiser than I, the more I've been been exposed to influences that thrust me to a more elevated way of considering aesthetics.

From meeting and indulging in the company of an assortment of deeply benevolent people, I've learned to value the traits of compassion and generosity as far more gorgeous than striking external lure. From sharing memories with artists of different genres, I have learned to effusively appreciate the pulchritude of creating something dazzling out of nothing. From family and teachers, I have been taught the magnitude of how beautiful it is to have access into the language of intellect. And from a vast variety of people, whether musicians or authors, friends or "freaks," I have discovered that without some level of undaunted, irrevocable strangeness, beauty cannot exist.

For what is beauty without creativity? Nothing really, just another face or a vacant name. And what is creativity without the strange, the bizarre? It ceases to live—it must die.

An idea I heard from a friend long ago has become ingrained in my way of viewing other people over time. This is the idea of objective beauty verses perceived beauty, and the difference between the two. Unfortunately the former type of beauty is the one which the world has adapted to and adopted as a lovechild. Objective beauty is characterized by what the general majority considers to be lovely or pleasing to look at, particularly as applied to people. Some stake the claim that this type of beauty does not exist, that beauty itself is too relative to narrow to such a contracted term, and in entirety, they would be right.

However, a young woman observed by a collection of people would typically receive similar responses according to her state of physical appeal. If she was, according to standards set by media and propaganda, considered physically beautiful, she would likely be lusted after by the male observers and either admired or envied (probably a combination of the two) by the female observers.

Alternately, if this young woman were, according to same standards, considered physically unattractive, she would likely be the subject of indifference or mocking of the male and female observers, possibly called demeaning names by both. Of course in this example, exceptions amongst the observers aren't taken into account, and the example in entirety is a generalization. Still, it being a generalization does not make it any less true, any less prominent in our society today. This is objective beauty. This type of beauty is sadistic and prejudiced, revealing the ugliness at the core of human nature. And all of us, no matter how good or just, have not failed to fall victim to it and abuse it in our daily lives.

Now perceived beauty is quite different. In a way it is ineffable, but I will do my best. Perceived beauty is unconditional, but relative to each person. In regard to humanity, it is the beauty that each individual discovers through knowing another and what they are capable of as well as, simply, what they are. Perceived beauty almost lives synonymous to love, because it is through love that people are able to discover and cherish this beauty in other humans. This type of beauty can't be altered by style or standards, comparison or the media. The loveliest thing of it is its consistency. Loving someone not for their face, but for their heart; sacrificing yourself for another, regardless of their flaws—perceived beauty is love.

Because real beauty is farfetched, fantastic dreams coming to life and emotions so real they're petrifying. Beauty is in relationships that tie people into intimacy and the loveliness of our world, in so many aspects. Dreams and feelings and relationships, the components of this earth, are all bizarre. Living—life— is bizarre.

Walking between the lines and following the commercial standards like life is a balance beam is the best way to short-circuit your potential, to eliminate every aspect of yourself that makes you unique, that others admire. Living only to the limit of normalcy will render you miserable. It's no wonder, in all honesty, that the people who deem themselves popular loathe and lash out at the rest, the different ones, the best. The popular people aren't fulfilling a quarter of their potential. What could be more unsatisfying?

The people who live their lives abstaining from their true nature, donning a plastic mask and mocking themselves and everyone else for that matter by pretending that any human actually is so artificial, are destined to be unsatisfied. These people like to live under the illusion that they are the sole focus of envy, while in turn, they themselves long to be just as real and free as the very souls they spend their days tormenting. Many outsiders think that they are envying the beautiful people, but in fact they are envying the artificial, and the artificial are envying them. Truly, it is the different people who are brilliant. And everyone, especially the popular ones, are able to distinguish this upon opening their eyes.

Aliens on their own planet,

Victim to the music molten, art impassioned pages,
White noise shrieks, and unearthed sages.
Like gasoline and flame making love underwater,
You blaze, Vivacious, forever the martyr.
Tangibly surreal, possessing sanity to the fraction,
They are paramour to the chain reaction.
Emotive souls, the lives they save
Shaping malleable art out of the desolate days
The others shudder in clandestine envy
At the nature of such an alien assembly
Draped in misery's coat, you solidify,
To not be you is to be Argus-eyed*[1]*.*
Static spirits, in tune to the heart,
Resilient to the deceptions who threaten to slash them apart.
Their eyes sheath passion, knowing they're one,
Their humanistic luminance this century's sun.

SMB

---

1 Argus is a symbol of envy from Greek Mythology.

Most people who have achieved fame through creation or accomplishment had to, at some point in his or her life, embrace the strangeness of who he or she was as an individual. In many cases, the people who are celebrated with stardom were once labeled the freaks in high school, deemed too unusual or original to fit into the popular crowd; likewise, the people who are the outsiders in high school, who live how they are despite what the crowd claims, are almost always the people who amount to any form of greatness later in life.

Less often do the popular teenagers amount to greatness, reigning as demigods during high school, but failing to accomplish anything with their lives once the four glory years have elapsed and faded. Many teenagers consistently forget this, but high school is a just a blip in the grand scheme of things. Instead of spending those four years sweating to please the masses, actually attempt to achieve something for yourself, something that will lead you somewhere relevant in life. We may be in high school now, but in a short matter of years, no more than four, most of those people will subsequently vanish from our lives, probably never again to be seen.

Don't waste your high school years striving to please people to the point where you dispose of your identity, not attempting to befriend those who allow you to grow as a person and not attempting to be who are for fear of what it will cost you. Yet the idea of passing through life pretending should cause greater alacrity than the state of expressing who you actually are. Many adults gaze back at high school, wrought with regret over the fact that they treated it more like a talent or fashion show than an opportunity to show the world what extraordinary human beings they were.

When you're different, even what others find simplistic is a struggle, and it's not possible to avoid the anguish of not understanding yourself among the others. On too many occasions I walked the crowded school hallways, feeling so agonizingly overwhelmed by the horrific din of the masses, nearly driven mad by their shallow words with hollow meanings. The most imperative of information for you to invoke when you feel this way is that you are amongst the few special ones. You are the one who holds true relevance amongst the pandemonium. Let them make you believe otherwise, and *they* are the victorious ones.

Fateful Flower

A single seed nestles within the warm and welcoming soil
The soil nurtures it and allows it to break through the surface
It emerges with such beauty, bringing life to all surrounding creation
No desolation dares go near this efflorescence
It flourishes with each coming day
Dripping with elegance, putting every blossoming rose to shame
Time's expedition flies by, rustling the petals of the flower in breeze.

Other flowers begin to develop around the floret
They bundle over top this delicate beauty
They veil the gorgeous plant from the rest of the world
Darkness casts down upon it from the shadows of the others.

The petals that were once soft and pure begin to wither away
The stem that once stood so strong relinquishes its vibrant color.

Yet the other flowers continue multiplying towards the sky,
Thorns of vanity and scorn swelling from their tenebrous stalks
Their roots thirst for the final remains of vivacity that the flower
possesses
The naïve flower relinquishes it willingly,
Wishing for nothing more than to please those that confine it
The thistles multiply, pushing toward the diminishing flower.
They grip the petiole that keeps it from collapsing to the earthy soil

They squeeze the existence from the once animated creature,
Uprooting the unloved flower.

The flower has come to its final day.
It drops to the ground with grace.
It will soon be forgotten.
It was never known.

Lindzy Nieman

Consider succumbing to the multitude's expectations suicide to your individuality and uniqueness. If you don't defend the distinctive traits that set you apart from others, then the others will slash you to shreds, leaving you with nothing but a negated existence and maimed self-esteem. If you relinquish traits of your identity to become something less peculiar for the sole purpose of merging into the crowd, then you are nothing greater than a follower.

I didn't use to defend my identity and I always attempted to fashion a mock persona in order to attract other people. Luckily for me, my strangeness always bled through the façade anyway.

However, the more I came to see the true characteristics of the people of that narcissist society, the more I began to see how stunning the less self-absorbed, more unorthodox people were. Once these people became involved in my life, I realized that I was too bizarre to ever blend into the popular scene and that I didn't truly want to be a player such an assembly anyway. Insecurity still plagued me, and prevented me from instantly emerging from my shell.

Music itself is the most emotive of liberators. In my darkest of days, I identify with the visceral lives of rock artists—the incisive human beings that possess the ability to weave stories through rhythm, stories so tragically dazzling and savagely human that they caused me to shudder in violent comprehension. To hear that song or lyric causes us to ache in reciprocality, and we are tied to their anguish; because we have lived those exact feelings and we have known that exact brand of suffering.

Exploring the works of authors and art makers whose creations illuminated the vitality of uniqueness and the appeal of the unusual people allowed me to come so much closer to myself. Overwhelming myself in expression of emotions through the veneer of theatre performance, I was taught to a greater extent the grasp I hold over my emotions and what can be created out of this control and lack of. I also met others—unconventional artists, of no particular genre—who sought to bring laughter and amusement to the lives of others with their antics; they weren't prejudice or judging in any shape or form, treating every type of person with acceptance, and to anyone criticized their bizarre lifestyle, they metaphorically shrugged, unaffected, and continued on. And, probably the most crucial to whom I am as a person today, I met the artists of no genre in particular; these were people who had already mastered what I still needed to comprehend about myself and about others.

Today, I fathom what I once only longed to grasp: the beauty of being someone that the popular people don't approve of me being. Not always am I concretely resolute in what I know to be profoundly true; I must be perpetually reasserted in my belief by God and by the people I identify with. But knowing with passion the vastness of what beauty lies within the so-called strange, I am tethered to ground myself to what is true and good.

My ignorance to the world is infinite in innumerable areas, and I could only fill few books with the little I *do* know about this life and its people. One and a half more years of high school gape at me, a black-hole of possibilities, downfalls, miracles, opportunities, and heartbreaks. But what I do know is that I refuse to walk between the lines, meandering through a web of self-defacing restrictions that are strung about in order to keep people in line. I will destroy the web and walk where I want to walk. I have so much more to discover, about myself, about humanity, about the rest of the world, and it makes no sense to waste time trying to please the majority, abiding by the accepted rules, and flinging myself at the feet of the popular clan like some kind of ignorant, moronic sacrifice to their oh-so-mundane glory. One real person is worth more than the entire lot of them. They are the artificial. They are arrogant and ludicrous in how they live to judge others. We are the differents, the *difference*. And we cause the change.

9. To Love the Rest

"When we treat people merely as they are, they will remain as they are. When we treat them as if they were what they should be, they will become what they should be. "
Thomas S. Monson

"There is nothing so rewarding as to make people realize that they are worthwhile in this world."
Bob Anderson

W*here are we now?* Where do we go from here? What is there to aspire to, to spend our lives seeking to accomplish? Is there any question more difficult than the one that inquires the purpose, the meaning of life? I can think of none. However, beginning with that question is an impossibly vast step to take, an inconceivable leap. There is an equally vital question that needs answering before that one, one even more essential, and it is this—*how am I going to live my life?*

The person who I was a few years ago no longer lives, existing only as a phantom of my present self. I used to be a cookie-cutter of a person; I stuck to the mold, diminishing myself into a disfigurement of my true form, revealing nothing that would establish a lasting impression. So strong was my desire to be liked and approved of, I gave nothing, shared nothing of myself, for what if the piece of myself that I relinquished were to be rejected?

I took no risks to allow people to get to know me, gave and presented nothing for people to like or dislike. For if I did, I would risk the chance of being broken like I'd been so often before. So, in turn, many people who didn't dislike me didn't like me either. How could they? All they knew of me was that I was a weirdo posing as a people pleaser, always trying relentlessly to say the right thing or act the correct way. It fatigued and discouraged me. *Why don't people like me?* I demanded, constantly, until the mental question became my redundant mantra. It took years—inanely long—for for me to discover the answer.

Before we gather the strength to start developing real relationships with the rest of the world, we live emotionally. I was a crippled human being. I wasn't a robot, but I acted the part. Inside, I shrieked with potential, with stunted purpose, but out of selfish fear, released only fragments of myself, if any of my personality at all. So what did people in turn do to me?

They excluded me, they ignored me, the lamentations drone on. For what was I, but a pretender, a coward? So much more, but only beneath the surface. No one was aware though, because I gave no one the chance to know anything of me truly, besides mundane facts lacking sentiment. This blatantly declared the apparent truth that I was afraid of life. Because I was afraid of life, of living. Though I'm not entirely fearless now, instead of obscuring myself beneath expectations, I am open with people and aim to entrust compassion to others, even when it's difficult to do so.

To live in fear is self-destructive, due to the truth that it squashes your potential by giving others nothing to love about you. By living this way, I succeeded in making myself entirely miserable. I felt suffocated from the rest of the world, excluded from most everything, everyone. And I was doing that to myself. But living in such a way not only stunted my own growth, but it gave nothing to others as well. The way I used to live was both completely self-defacing and wholly selfish.

Each person is a universe within themselves, a unique entity. Every person has the exceptional power—sadly so seldom utilized—to change someone's day, someone's life, by opening themselves up to another. For those you are in close contact with, offer them your attention and affection, because more often than not, a person longs, more than anything else, for another who cares enough to listen. For those you aren't in close contact with, greet them with compassion and friendliness, as simplistic, kind actions may often turn the tide in someone's day.

Being innately shy, I started as simply as by smiling at people, people who didn't seem to care for me, people I didn't even know. And when I smiled at these people, who knows how they accepted the gesture? They could possibly have thought, *Wow, I really needed that on a day like this.* They also could have thought, *Why the hell is she smiling at me? I don't know her.* Either way, so what?

From that point on, people stopped neither liking nor disliking me. Instead, they generally viewed me in either a positive or negative way, not an indifferent manner, as I was regarded in before; this is the way it should be. Someone disliking you doesn't mean anything toward your character, after all, so it shouldn't be feared so, be a thing that should be sought to avoid at all costs. All it means in itself is that *that* specific person and you are different types of people, with traits and ideas that don't coincide well. Again I say, so *what*? The people who dislike you aren't the people who matter in your personal life. As people, though, they deserve to be treated well, regardless of how they treat you, something that is not always easy to do and that is not often exercised in today's society.

Something to remind yourself is that love is characterized by seeking to be compassionate to all people. To be kind to those who are like you or who you share close relation with does not require any heart. If a person is staggeringly different than you, if they dislike you, or if you don't think they are a good person, it shouldn't have effect on your treatment of them. Still give these people a chance, give them small acts of kindness, for it is not unkindness that changes people to be kind.

You don't have to cease to defend yourself, others, and what you believe in; simply do so without entertaining bitterness or malice, hostility or arrogance. By being different, you hold the responsibility of regarding and interacting with your oppressors differently than they regard and interact with you. While society today condones returning violence with violence and lashing out hatred upon those who hate you, these behaviors only circulate endlessly in a vehement cycle. Growth may only be allowed when this cycle is allowed to be broken. Who better to allow this change to be instigated than those who know from raw experience the impact that unkindness can have on people and the sorrow that hatred unleashes?

Despite the pertinence of striving to live by giving unconditional kindness, in your personal life, the people who dislike you aren't the ones who hold true value. The friendships that allow you depth are the relationships that are truly prevalent. And only once I was real with myself did I find these inimitable people. And that is the greatest reward you will receive for sharing your heart with others, all others. You will eventually, if not immediately, receive in return. Love, compassion, and uniqueness shared with the right people will be returned to you.

I personally believe that God is the standard of goodness, the example that we follow when we love other people. And He made us to hold each other together; without opening up to others, we will never be granted the opportunity to find those people that we desperately need. There are few greater travesties.

Meeting the weird, wonderful people who identified with who I was as a person is what truly allowed me transformation. Being involved in these true friendships, I found that it grew easier for me to be honest with myself as a person. Strengthened and supported by these new-found friends, I could engage in conversation with people who I didn't know, a feat that previously had terrified me, and in doing so reveal my true personality to them, a task that used to be—for me—unthinkable. Instead of solely being concerned with what people thought of me, I shelved this thought and instead fastened my focus on treating others with kindness.

More often than I am securely confident in whom I am, I am doubting and disliking myself. No matter what I know about who I should be, I am utterly human and have warped self-esteem and insecurities galore. Nothing will ever change this. What *has* changed since *I* changed is that I do not loath, or even hate, myself anymore.

You have to care about yourself before you try to love other people, or else you will end up hurting someone without even attempting to. No matter how confident you are in yourself, you will at some point (most likely many points) doubt what you know and who you are as an individual.

That's why everyone needs an example to follow, a leader who goes to a place beyond where you ever dared of venturing yourself and creates a space where you can be who you are without restrictions. Musicians are an example of people who demolish boundaries and allow people to find beauty in the places they need it the most. These artists boldly lay out their souls before the world through songs, pieces of themselves that are to be savagely assaulted or fiercely adored. Some say musicians are eternally heartbroken and I agree—to give so much away and to never be fully accepted is an indescribable ache. But what they give, they give so much; they bring brilliance to people's lives, making their days worth living when there doesn't seem to be much else to survive for.

To imagine a life without music is unfathomable to me, and agonizing to think of. But you don't have to be a musician, a star, or a person of fame to contribute to peoples' lives in ways that they will always treasure. Every person has the potential to permanently change the lives of others, for better or for worse. We do it all the time—every single day.

You have indisputably, on more than one occasion, positively impacted someone in a way that changes his or her life permanently; you also have possibly saved someone from demise, are quite possibly the reason that someone today is alive and not the alternative. And, terrifying as the thought is, you also have broken at least one person's heart. Sometimes the impact, whether positive or negative, that we have on others we inflict involuntarily; however, it is up to us to decide in what way we want to strive to impact the lives of people around us.

Being different is more than a name, an idea, or a way of life. If that were all it was, then the different people would merely be a more interesting version of the popular clique. Being different means holding a different perspective than others and having an elevated perception of the world. Being different means imparting kindness and honesty not only to your friends and people like you, but also to the other ones, your opposites—in the case of the different people, the popular people.

If you are different, you aren't satisfied with the world as it is, where cruelty and self-consumed ambition are custom and an act of selfless kindness is strangeness, a cause for suspicion. Vanity, pride, and envy attempt again and again to starve bizarreness and beauty out of existence, but if people exist who know what in life is relevant and deserves defending, this can never happen.

To love the rest is the way to salvage what is real in this world. Popularity is nothing but a hollow word and normalcy is nothing but an illusion. Nothing implicit sets the standard for what is normal, thus proving that normalcy is unreal—just like the lives of those who are masquerading as being normal. This world is overrun with madness, mad people with mad ideas, some in intent of salvaging good and many in aim of raising evil; life itself is is divinely chaotic. Little in life makes sense. So love it all. Love the world. Love what is good and lovely. Love the real people. And knowing what you know, love the popular people. The day they discover they are living an illusion, they are going to need all the love that you are able to give.

www.ingramcontent.com/pod-product-compliance
Lightning Source LLC
Chambersburg PA
CBHW021836020426
42334CB00014B/652